The Demon Lover

A Chilling Wartime Ghost Story of
Trauma and Return

A Modern Translation

Adapted for the Contemporary Reader

Elizabeth Bowen

Translated by Tim Zengerink

Table of Contents

Preface - Message to the Reader

What If You Could Help Rebuild the Greatest Library in Human History?

Thousands of years ago, the Library of Alexandria stood as the crown jewel of human achievement — a sanctuary where the collected wisdom of every known civilization was gathered, preserved, and shared freely.

And then, it was lost.

Through fire, conquest, and the slow erosion of time, humanity lost not just books — but ideas, dreams, discoveries, and stories that could have changed the world forever.

Today, the Library of Alexandria lives again — and you are invited to be a part of its restoration.

Our mission is simple yet profound:

To rebuild the greatest library the world has ever known, and to translate all timeless works into every language and dialect, so that no seeker of knowledge is ever left behind again.

By joining our movement to rebuild the modern Library of Alexandria, you become part of an unprecedented mission:

- **Unlimited Access to the Greatest Audiobooks & eBooks Ever Written:**

  Instantly explore thousands of legendary works—Plato, Shakespeare, Jane Austen, Leo Tolstoy, and countless more. All instantly available to read or listen, placing a complete literary universe at your fingertips.

- **Beautiful Paperback & Deluxe Editions at Printing Cost**

  Own any title as an elegant paperback, deluxe hardcover, or stunning collectible boxset—offered to you at true printing cost, delivered straight to your door. Build your personal Library of Alexandria, crafted for beauty, built for durability, and worthy of proud display.

- **Fresh Translations for Modern Readers—in Every Language & Dialect**

  Enjoy timeless masterpieces reimagined in clear, contemporary language—no more outdated phrases or obscure references. Alongside the original versions, we're tirelessly translating these classics into every language and dialect imaginable, ensuring accessibility and understanding across cultures and generations.

- **Join a Global Renaissance of Literature & Knowledge**

    You directly support expanding our library, publishing deluxe editions at true cost, translating works into all global languages, and bringing humanity's greatest stories to people everywhere. By joining today, you're not just preserving a legacy of masterpieces; you set in motion a powerful wave of literary accessibility.

Become a Torchbearer of Knowledge.

Join us for free now at **LibraryofAlexandria.com**

Together, we will ensure that the light of human wisdom never fades again.

With gratitude and a shared love of knowledge,

The Modern Library of Alexandria Team

Visit:

www.libraryofalexandria.com

Or scan the code below:

Introduction

Ghosts of War, Memory,
and the Price of Repression

Elizabeth Bowen's The Demon Lover, first published in 1945 during the final throes of the Second World War, is a short story of extraordinary psychological depth and symbolic resonance. At barely a few pages in length, it compresses within itself the emotional trauma of a world in collapse, the unhealed wounds of the First World War, and the chilling persistence of the past. More than a ghost story, it is a reflection on the cost of forgetting, the spectral weight of memory, and the uncanny return of promises unkept.

Set in war-damaged London, The Demon Lover follows Mrs. Kathleen Drover, a middle-aged woman who returns to her shuttered family home to collect belongings during a break in the Blitz. The house, vacant and musty, is thick with silence and unease. There she finds an unexpected letter placed on the hall table—a letter with no stamp, no signature, and a chilling reminder of a promise she made to a soldier twenty-five years ago, one presumed dead in the trenches of the First World War. As Kathleen descends into confusion and dread, the story unfolds as a masterful study in psychological unraveling and supernatural ambiguity. In the final lines, she enters a taxi—a vehicle that may be her escape, or her doom.

Though often categorized as a supernatural tale, The Demon Lover refuses easy categorization. It is as much a wartime allegory as it is a ghost story. The demon lover may be a spirit returned from the dead, a hallucination, or the embodiment of trauma that has never been resolved. Bowen, a master of modernist technique and psychological subtlety, leaves the story open to multiple readings, each more disturbing than the last. What remains certain is the atmosphere: tense, claustrophobic, and laced with dread.

In this introduction, we will explore The Demon Lover in three interwoven threads: its grounding in wartime psychology and modernist literature; its subversion of gothic tropes and archetypes; and its deeper themes of repression, guilt, and the return of the repressed. Through this lens, Bowen's story reveals itself to be not just a tale of terror, but a profound meditation on the unseen forces that shape identity, history, and human fate.

Modern War and Modern Ghosts: Trauma in the Shadow of Conflict

To understand the full power of The Demon Lover, it must be situated within the historical context of its creation. Written during World War II but set during an air raid reprieve in London, the story takes place amid the ruins of empire, both physical and psychological. The house that Kathleen reenters is a symbol of this ruin—a domestic space cracked by bombs, emptied of life, and suspended in time. Her return is not a homecoming. It is an encounter with absence.

This environment is critical to the story's horror. Bowen was deeply attuned to the emotional aftermath of war, especially the lingering, insidious effects of unresolved trauma. Kathleen is not simply frightened by a letter. She is destabilized by the return of something she has spent decades burying. The unnamed soldier—her demon lover—represents a past that refuses to be forgotten. He may be dead, but his promise still holds. And Bowen, with her characteristic restraint, never clarifies if this figure is truly supernatural or a projection of Kathleen's guilt and denial.

The story therefore becomes an exploration of post-traumatic haunting. Kathleen's life, like so many others in interwar England, was built upon the assumption that the horrors of the Great War could be placed behind them. But the Blitz—a second, more immediate apocalypse—exposes the fragility of that denial. The past returns, not only in memory, but in form. The letter is not just a narrative device. It is a summons.

This motif aligns Bowen with a tradition of modernist writers who used ghostly or psychological motifs to represent internal fracture: Virginia Woolf, Henry James, and T.S. Eliot. Like them, Bowen saw the uncanny not as a departure from realism but as its deepening. In the irrational and the spectral, she found ways to articulate the subconscious toll of history. Kathleen is haunted not because she believes in ghosts, but because she believed she had escaped them.

The Gothic Reimagined:
Domestic Dread and Feminine Confinement

On the surface, The Demon Lover borrows many of the conventions of gothic literature: an old house, a letter from the past, an unnamed suitor, a woman in distress, and an ambiguous supernatural force. But Bowen reworks these elements through a distinctly modern lens. The setting is not a castle or a forest, but a bourgeois London townhouse. The heroine is not a naïve maiden, but a middle-aged woman with a husband, children, and a socially constructed identity. The danger she faces is not overt, but psychological, latent, and eerily familiar.

The result is a story where dread accumulates not through action, but through atmosphere. Every room in the house seems to whisper. Every silence becomes deafening. Kathleen's perception of time begins to fracture. She sees reflections, misremembers locations, and experiences reality as though submerged in water. This disorientation is not just atmospheric—it is structural. Bowen uses short, clipped sentences, abrupt shifts, and subtle repetition to induce the sensation of entrapment. The reader, like Kathleen, becomes unsure of what is real.

Kathleen's gender is also central to the story's power. The demon lover is not merely a ghost; he is a claimant. He represents a promise Kathleen made not as a woman in love, but as a young girl pressured by the tropes of romantic martyrdom. The letter does not address her current identity. It speaks to the girl she was, a self she thought she had shed. Bowen here critiques the cultural expectation that women remain bound to their youthful romantic promises—even if those promises are impossible, coercive, or deadly.

The taxi, in this reading, becomes a gothic vehicle: a modern-day hearse, a chariot of abduction. Kathleen's entry into it may be her final surrender to the past, or her collapse into madness. We are not told where it goes. We only see her face, gripped with fear, as the doors lock and the narrative ends.

This ambiguity is crucial. Gothic fiction has always concerned itself with boundaries—between life and death, sanity and madness, inside and outside. Bowen, however, refuses to resolve these tensions. She does not offer exorcism or escape. She simply closes the door, and leaves us with the sound of a taxi moving through a city of ruins.

Memory, Guilt, and the Return of the Repressed

Perhaps the most enduring interpretation of The Demon Lover lies in the realm of psychoanalysis. Kathleen is not simply a woman stalked by a ghost. She is a woman who has split herself in two—who has built a life on the negation of a formative trauma. The soldier she once loved disappeared in the cataclysm of World War I. She moved on, married, had children, and entered a social world that demanded forgetfulness. But repression, as Freud argued, does not delete. It stores. And in Bowen's hands, it waits.

The story functions, then, as a case study in the return of the repressed. The house, locked and undisturbed, is a physical manifestation of Kathleen's unconscious. The letter appears not because it was sent, but because something inside her has surfaced. Her reaction is not grief, but panic. She does not process or reflect. She flees.

This response speaks to a larger critique embedded in the story: that British society—particularly among the middle class—failed to truly mourn the Great War. Instead, it built a fragile normalcy upon silence. Women like Kathleen were expected to adapt, to marry, to mother, to rebuild. But they were never allowed to speak of what they lost, or who they became in the process.

Bowen, through her ghost story, gives voice to that silenced grief. The demon lover is not just a man. He is a metaphor for all that was buried: the violence, the longing, the guilt of survival. And in this way, the story becomes not just an individual haunting, but a national one.

The final scene—the locked taxi, the vanished driver, the silent journey—is both literal and symbolic.

It may depict a woman abducted by a ghost, or a woman driven into breakdown. But it also depicts something larger: the way in which the past, unacknowledged, reclaims the present. Kathleen is not taken because she sinned. She is taken because she forgot. And in Bowen's world, forgetting is not forgiveness. It is permission.

The Demon Lover endures because it does not try to explain itself. Like the best ghost stories, it leaves space for interpretation, for silence, for dread. It does not tell us what happened. It shows us what happens when history knocks at the door.

And we answer, thinking it will go away.

The Demon Lover

Near the end of her day in London, Mrs. Drover visited her closed-up house to pick up a few things she needed. Some items were hers, and some belonged to her family, who had gotten used to living in the countryside. It was late August, and the day had been hot and rainy. Now, the trees along the sidewalk sparkled in the thick, yellow light of the afternoon sun. Dark clouds were already piling up behind the buildings, and their outlines stood out sharply. The street, once familiar to her, now felt strange and empty—like a place that hadn't been used for a long time. A cat weaved through the railings, but no person seemed to notice her return.

Balancing some packages under her arm, she slowly turned her key in the stiff lock, then pushed the warped door open with her knee. As she stepped inside, a wave of stale air met her.

The hallway was dark since the stairway window had been boarded up. But she noticed one door slightly open and walked quickly through it into the room, opening the large window to let in light. Looking around, she felt more unsettled than she expected. She noticed small signs of the life she once lived here: a yellow stain from smoke on the white marble above the fireplace, a ring left by a vase on the writing desk, and a dent in the wallpaper where the door handle used to hit when the door swung open. The piano had been taken away for storage, and the floor where it used to sit now had marks that looked like scratches. Although not much dust had gotten in, everything seemed covered in a thin layer of stillness. The room smelled cold and unused, with the only airflow coming from the chimney.

Mrs. Drover set her packages down on the writing desk and headed upstairs—the things she needed were in a bedroom drawer.

She had been worried about the condition of the house. The part-time caretaker she shared with neighbors was on vacation and wasn't expected back yet. Even when he was around, he didn't visit often, and she wasn't sure she trusted him. There were cracks left from the last bombing that she wanted to keep an eye on, though there wasn't much she could actually do about them.

As she reached the hallway again, she saw a patch of light fall across the floor. She froze and stared at the hallway table. There, lying on it, was a letter addressed to her.

At first, she assumed the caretaker had returned. But the house had been locked up—who would have dropped off a letter? It wasn't a flyer or a bill. All her mail was sent to her country address. And even if the caretaker had come back, he wouldn't have known she'd be in London today—this visit had been a surprise. She felt irritated that the letter had been left there in the dust. Frustrated, she picked it up. It had no stamp. Still, she thought, if it was truly important, they would have found another way to reach her...

Without reading it yet, she quickly took the letter upstairs. She didn't look at the handwriting until she had opened the blinds. The window faced the garden, and the dark shapes of the trees and messy lawn looked like they were already fading into shadows. She didn't want to read the letter—not just because it felt like someone had invaded her space, but also because it felt like whoever left it didn't respect her. Still, with the pressure of the coming storm in the air, she finally read the short message.

Dear Kathleen,

I'm sure you remember—today is our special day, the one we agreed on. The time since then has felt both long and short. Because everything is still the same, I'm counting on you to keep your word.

I felt a bit let down when you left London, but I believed you'd return in time. So, I'll be there at the time we decided.

See you soon…

K.

Mrs. Drover looked at the date on the letter—it was today's. Her hands shook as she dropped it onto the bed, then quickly picked it up again to look more closely at the handwriting. Her lips, still slightly tinted with old lipstick, began to lose color. Feeling the change in her face, she walked to the mirror, cleared a small spot, and looked at herself with both urgency and fear.

She saw a forty-four-year-old woman staring back. Her wide eyes peeked out from under a hat she had thrown on without much care. She hadn't freshened up since she had tea alone earlier that day. The pearl necklace her husband gave her when they got married now hung loosely on her thinner neck, slipping into the V of a soft pink sweater her sister had knitted last fall by the fire. Her usual look was one of quiet worry, with a hint of acceptance. Ever since the birth of her third child, which had left her seriously ill, she sometimes had a small twitch in her mouth. Still, she always managed to seem strong and calm.

She turned away from the mirror as quickly as she had gone to it. Then she walked over to the chest, unlocked it, opened the lid, and knelt to search inside. But as the rain started crashing against the windows, she couldn't stop herself from glancing back at the empty bed where the letter still lay. Through the downpour, she heard the church clock chime six times. Her fear grew with each slow ring.

"The time we planned... Oh no," she whispered. "What time? How could I know? It's been twenty-five years..."

She thought back to when she was a young girl, talking to a soldier in the garden. She had never clearly seen his face—it was dark, and they were saying goodbye under a tree. At that moment, it felt like she had never really seen him at all. She had reached out now and then, just to make sure he was still there. Each time, he would press her hand—not gently—against one of the buttons on his uniform. The way the button cut into her palm was the main thing she remembered. It was near the end of his leave from France, and all she could do was hope he'd go soon. It was August 1916.

He hadn't kissed her. He hadn't even held her. The cold way he looked at her made her feel nervous, even afraid. She imagined strange lights flashing in place of his eyes. When she turned away and looked back toward the house, she saw the warm light glowing through the living room window between the tree branches. She took a deep breath, waiting for the moment she could run back to her mother and sister and cry, "What should I do? He's gone."

He heard her gasp and asked calmly,

"Are you feeling cold?"

"You're going so far away," she said.

"Not as far as you think."

"I don't understand."

"You don't need to," he said. "You will. You know what we promised."

"But that was—what if something happens to you?"

"I'll return," he said. "Sooner or later. Don't forget. Just wait for me."

A minute later, she was finally able to run across the quiet lawn. She looked through the window at her mother and sister, who hadn't seen her yet. Even then, she could feel that strange promise standing between her and everyone else in the world. No other promise could have made her feel so alone, so far from everyone. She couldn't have made a more chilling commitment.

When her fiancé was reported missing a few months later and believed to be dead, Kathleen stayed calm. Her family stood by her and praised her for being brave. Since they barely knew the man, they didn't feel much grief and hoped she'd move on in a year or two. If it had only been about sadness, maybe she could have. But her pain ran deeper than that—she felt completely out of place in the world.

She didn't push away new suitors—none came. For years, no man seemed interested. As she approached her thirties, she started to share her family's worries about her future. She began trying harder, putting herself out there. By thirty-two, she was incredibly relieved to be courted by William Drover. They got married and settled in a quiet, leafy area of Kensington. That's where the years passed, her children were born, and they lived until the bombs of another war forced them to leave.

As Mrs. Drover, her life was small and routine. She told herself that no one was watching anymore.

The writer of the letter—whoever or whatever they were—had sent her only one thing: a threat. Mrs. Drover couldn't keep kneeling with her back to the room, so she stood up and sat on a stiff chair with its back pressed against the wall. The bedroom, once hers, now felt unused and distant. The whole house felt like a broken cup—something that had once held memories but now had nothing left inside. And it was at this exact moment of weakness that the letter writer had chosen to strike. The silence in the house erased all the years of familiar voices, routines, and footsteps. Outside, through the shut windows, she could only hear the rain tapping on the rooftops.

Trying to calm down, she told herself it was just her nerves. She even closed her eyes for a few seconds and pretended she'd imagined the letter. But when she looked again—it was still there on the bed.

She refused to think about anything supernatural. Who even knew she would be visiting the house today? Somehow, someone did. If the caretaker had returned, he wouldn't have expected her. He would've taken the letter and mailed it to her later. There was no sign that he had been in the house. But if not him—then who?

Letters don't just appear on dusty tables in empty houses. They don't walk there on their own. Someone had to place it there. But only the caretaker had a key. Still, if someone really wanted to, they could have found another way in. And maybe she wasn't alone now. Maybe someone was downstairs, waiting. Waiting for what? For "the hour we agreed on"? At least she knew that hour wasn't six—she had just heard it strike.

She stood up and quickly locked the door.

What mattered now was getting out. Not running away—but catching her train. She had come here for a reason, to pick up some things for her husband, kids, and sister. She couldn't go back without them. She returned to the chest and began gathering the items quickly, though her hands were shaky. With her shopping bags too, it would be too much to carry on foot—she would need a taxi. The idea of calling one gave her some comfort. Just the thought of hearing the car engine running outside brought her back to herself.

I'll call a taxi, she thought. It can't get here fast enough. I'll walk down calmly through the hall. I'll ring—

But no, the phone was disconnected.

Frustrated, she yanked at a knot she had tied wrong.

The idea of running… He was never kind to me, she thought. Not really. I don't remember him being kind at all. Mom used to say he didn't care about me. He just wanted me. That wasn't love. That wasn't caring. Why did I promise him anything? What did he say or do to make me agree? I can't remember—

But suddenly, she could.

The memories hit so hard it felt like the twenty-five years had just disappeared. She looked at the palm of her hand, half-expecting to see the mark the button had left. She remembered everything he said and did, and how that whole week in August had felt like she wasn't even herself. Everyone had told her that at the time. She remembered it all—except for one thing. His face. It was just a blank, like acid had burned it off a photo.

So even if he was nearby, she wouldn't recognize him. And you can't run from someone you don't expect to see.

What mattered now was getting to the taxi before any clock struck the right hour—whatever that was. She'd slip down the street, cut through the square, and get to the main road. She'd ride back in the taxi, safe. She'd bring the driver inside with her to help carry the bags. That thought gave her strength. She unlocked the door, stepped onto the landing, and listened.

Nothing. But then, in that deep silence, she felt a breeze on her face—air moving up from the basement. Someone was down there. Someone was quietly opening a door or window.

The rain had stopped. The sidewalk was damp and shiny as she slowly stepped outside. The empty houses across the street stared back at her with broken windows. She headed toward the main road and tried not to look behind her. The silence in the city, made worse by war damage, was so deep that no one could have followed her without being heard. As she neared the edge of the square where people still lived, she realized how fast she was walking—and forced herself to slow down.

Two buses passed each other calmly. Women, a baby stroller, a few bikers, and a man pushing a cart moved along like normal. Life was going on. At the corner, the taxi line should be—and was—still there. Only one taxi tonight. But it looked like it was already waiting just for her. As she walked up from behind, the driver started the engine without even turning to look. She was out of breath as she grabbed the door handle— just then, the church clock struck seven.

The taxi was facing the main road, so it had to turn around to get back to her house. She had already settled into her seat when she realized something strange: she hadn't told the driver where to go. She leaned forward and tapped on the glass panel between them.

The driver slowed almost to a stop, turned, and slid the panel open. The jolt pushed her forward until her face was nearly pressed against the glass. For what felt like forever, she stared into the driver's eyes, only inches away.

Mrs. Drover's mouth opened, but no sound came out for a moment. Then she began to scream—loudly—and hit the glass with her gloved hands. But the taxi sped up, racing without mercy into the dark, empty streets, carrying her away.

Thank You for Reading

Dear Reader,

We hope this timeless classic has sparked your imagination and enriched your literary journey. Now that you've turned the final page, we want to share a vision for the future of reading—one where every classic you've ever wanted to explore is at your fingertips, in a format that best suits your life.

We'd like to invite you to gain immediate, unlimited digital & audiobook access to hundreds of the most treasured literary classics ever written—along with the option to secure deluxe paperback, hardcover & box set editions at printing cost. Together, we can spark a new global literary renaissance alongside our small, independent publishing house called "The Library of Alexandria."

Thousands of years ago, the Library of Alexandria stood as a beacon of knowledge—until it was lost to history. We aim to reignite that spirit of preservation and discovery right now, in the modern age—only this time, it's accessible to all, in every language and every format.

Picture a world where every timeless classic, novel, poem, or philosophical treatise is not only available to read but also updated for today's readers—modernized, translated into any language or dialect, and ready to enjoy in any format you choose, whether that is in an eBook, audiobook, paperback, or deluxe hardcover & box set version a printing cost.

By joining our movement to rebuild the modern Library of Alexandria, you become part of an unprecedented mission to offer:

- **Unlimited Audiobook & eBook Access** to the **Greatest Classics of All Time**

  Instantly explore thousands of legendary works, from Plato and Shakespeare to Jane Austen and Leo Tolstoy. All are instantly ready to read or listen to, giving you a complete literary universe at your fingertips.

- **Paperback & Deluxe Editions at Printing Costs:**

  Purchase any title in a paperback, deluxe hardbound, or deluxe boxset edition at printing costs, shipped right to your doorstep. Curate your personal library of Alexandria with editions worthy of display— crafted to last, designed to captivate, and delivered straight to your door.

- **Modern translations for Contemporary Readers in all languages and dialects**

  Discover a vast selection of classics reimagined in clear, current language—no more struggling with outdated phrases or obscure references. Next to the original versions, we aim to offer translations in as many languages and dialects as possible.

  As we continue our translation efforts and add new languages, readers everywhere can connect with these works as if they were written today. By bridging linguistic divides, you're contributing to ensuring that these timeless stories become more meaningful, accessible, and inspiring for people across the globe.

- **Your Personal Library of Alexandria:**

  Over the months and years, you'll curate a unique physical archive of classics—each volume a testament to your taste, curiosity, and love of knowledge. It's not just about owning books—it's about curating a cultural legacy you'll cherish and pass down for generations to come.

- **Join a Global Literary Renaissance:**

  Your support fuels an ongoing mission: allowing us to reinvest in offering deluxe print editions (including special boxsets) at their true cost, broaden the range of available formats and translations, and extend the reach of these works to new audiences worldwide. By joining today, you're not just preserving a legacy of masterpieces; you set in motion a powerful wave of literary accessibility.

We are more than a publisher—we're a movement, and we can't do it alone. Your support lets us scale our mission, preserving and reimagining history's greatest works for tomorrow's readers.

Become a Torchbearer of knowledge.

Thank you for picking up this book and allowing us into your literary journey. As you turn the pages, know that you're part of something larger: a global effort to keep these stories alive, share their wisdom across borders and generations, and spark a true cultural revival for the modern era.

If this resonates with you—please consider taking the next step by visiting:

www.libraryofalexandria.com

With gratitude and a shared love of knowledge,

The Modern Library of Alexandria Team

Visit:

www.libraryofalexandria.com

Or scan the code below: